Introduction

This is the story of *Merlin*, the last of the famous Compound locomotives of the former Great Northern Railway (Ireland).

The Compounds were built in 1932 to handle the increasingly heavy express passenger trains between Dublin and Belfast. The five locomotives quickly established a reputation for hard work and their popularity increased when they were the first to be painted blue in the late 1930s. All survived into the 1960s, most still able to do the job they were built for.

Rejected by two railway companies but rescued to live on in a museum, *Merlin* has been brought back to life in a most remarkable way. She is now enjoying a new lease of life hauling steam excursions organised by the Railway Preservation Society of Ireland (RPSI).

Most of the story is told in the pictures that follow, but first a bit of background.

It is an oft-told tale of how the Great Northern desperately wanted to get a locomotive more powerful than the S class 4-4-0s. The Ss already had superheating and there was little that could be done to make them even better than they were.

To explain quickly what superheating is about, we need to start with the (probably obvious) statement that steam is generated in a boiler under pressure and gathers at the boiler's highest point, the dome. There, the regulator controls the flow of steam to the cylinders where the steam is suddenly released from its compressed state. The pent-up energy of both pressure and temperature is converted into motion by the piston in the cylinder and the movement eventually turns the wheels.

In this system, the steam is taken from being in direct contact with the boiling water and is said to be saturated; some locomotive men call it "wet steam".

At the turn of the century, locomotive designers thought that they could get more work out of steam if they could heat it again — or superheat it — so that it entered the cylinders at the highest possible temperature. Superheating raises the temperature of steam (at 175 lbs per square inch) from 377° F (192°C) to 600°F (315°C). You can see why some locomotive men have referred to superheated steam as "dry", or even "burnt", steam.

As a result of superheating, the work done in the cylinders is increased by the equivalent of an additional 25% by volume. Raising the boiler pressure brings about an even bigger increase in volume. As you might expect, superheating made quite an impact.

The natural development of the GNR's fleet of 4-4-0s would be a 2-6-0 or a 4-6-0. But the engineers had set their hearts against a 2-6-0, probably because such a locomotive had a very poor stability record on the Southern Railway (England). Of course, the Great Southern Railways (the forerunner of CIE) had been running locomotives of this wheel arrangement in the Irish Free State since 1925, with some success, but the Dundalk Drawing Office remained unconvinced.

In Issue No 25 of *Five Foot Three*, the magazine of the RPSI, Paddy Mallon has explored the reasons for the Great Northern not adopting a 4-6-0. Essentially it came down a question of whether or not the thing could be fitted into Dundalk Works. The bottom line was that it couldn't. Walls would have to be moved, shops relocated, cranes and traverser replaced and all sorts of other bother and expense endured for the sake of a few locomotives.

Elsewhere, the Civil Engineer was about to rebuild the Boyne Viaduct so that heavier locomotives could use it. The Great Northern already had the SG3 goods locomotives that were too heavy to cross it. With the prospect of raising the maximum axle load from 17 to 21 tons, the Great Northern's Locomotive Department looked for a way of getting the maximum benefit from the increase.

The Mechanical Engineer, George T. Glover, had come from the North Eastern Railway's Darlington Works in 1912 and was familiar with the principles of compounding. Compounds had been very common on the Northern Counties Committee (NCC) at one time but were no longer in the ascendant there. Two other Irish lines had experimented with compounding before: the Belfast & County Down and the GSWR. On the latter, Aspinall had concluded that compounding was no better and no worse than simple working. Times had moved on since then and Glover was convinced that a combination of high boiler pressure and compounding would do the trick. In France particularly, pressures of 250 pounds per square inch were now common enough, yet many Irish locomotives were pressed to only 175 or even 160 lbs. The S class had recently gone up to 200 lbs with a 10% saving in coal consumption, so there may be hope yet.

Maybe it should be explained here, too, that in a compound locomotive the steam is used twice. It is, of course, superheated on its way from the regulator to the cylinders, and first passes through a conventional piston valve into the high pressure cylinder. It is exhausted from there, via a steam chest and two sets of slide valves, into the two low pressure cylinders where yet more work is extracted from it. The exhaust from the chimney is from each of the low pressure cylinders — to the observer or listener, the high pressure cylinder is virtually silent. In practice when starting away, the live steam is admitted to the steam chest and into each of the low pressure cylinders. Once the train is well under way, the change over to compounding is made by closing the regulator and opening it again so that the live steam, direct from the superheaters, is directed into the high pressure cylinder only. There is a noticeable drop in the noise from the chimney when this happens, which is all the more disconcerting for the locomotive can be felt to be pulling even more strongly.

Glover sent locomotive inspectors to England to travel on the footplates of LMS 4-4-0 Compounds, like the preserved No. 1000 in the National Railway Museum. They travelled over the Carlisle to Glasgow line and on the Settle and Carlisle, as well as the Midland route from Manchester to St. Pancras. They were very impressed with what they saw.

So it was that Beyer Peacock in Manchester were asked to build five three-cylinder compounds. The major dimensions are set out on the inside back cover of this book. In these locomotives the one high pressure cylinder was located between the frames and two low pressures mounted outside. The valve gear for all three cylinders was inside, driven off the crank axle of the leading drivers.

The new locomotives had many firsts to their credit — they were the first completely new design of compound in the British Isles for thirty years. They were the only 4-4-0s in the British Isles to work at 250 psi. They had the highest pressure of any conventional Irish locomotive, and were the first three-cylinder locomotives in Ireland. They were claimed to have the longest coupling rods in the world at 10 feet 8 inches, but are reputed to have been pipped at the post by a Scandinavian locomotive (10 feet $8^{1/8}$" inches!).

The new locomotives were numbered 83 to 87 and named after birds of prey, the plates being cast in Dundalk. They were 83 *Eagle*; 84 *Falcon*; 85 *Merlin*; 86 *Peregrine*; and 87 *Kestrel*. Despite rumours to the contrary, 85 has nothing to do with the magician of Arthurian legend — even if you think they are magic engines!

The locomotives were delivered without tenders. Dundalk built two new 3500 gallon tenders and three others were taken from SG3 0-6-0s. Later these tenders had the side sheets extended by additional curved plates to increase the coal capacity. The well known Beyer Peacock photograph of No. 87 in 'shop grey' livery is a clever fake. The nameplate was added after the photograph and the tender was from the photograph of SG3 0-6-0, No. 202 built in 1921.

When new, the locomotives had round-topped boilers and the first livery applied to the engines was black lined with a $1/4$" red line, later enlarged to $1/2$".

Almost at once, the locomotives were sent out on the greatly accelerated trains of the summer 1932 timetable with its 60 mph start to stop timings between Dublin and Dundalk, and heavier loads all round, not to mention trimming about 15 minutes off the running time between the capitals. Some observers feel that they did not get a chance to get run-in beforehand. Certainly they were plagued with hot boxes and hot connecting rods. After two frantic years, the maintenance bills demanded a reduction in pressure to 200 psi and the boilers were ready for retubing!

Then in 1936 came the introduction of the blue livery now so familiar to many of us. Fred Graham recalls someone at Adelaide dismissing it as "the same colour as a farm cart!" Whatever about the cart, the new livery made the locomotives stand out. Maybe it was a bit too good at doing that. When the Works had several of them waiting for repairs (after the Ss were renewed), they covered them in tarpaulins so as not to attract attention to all the big engines that were out of action.

During the Second World War, the Compounds were asked to haul prodigious loads. They were seen taking twelve or even fourteen bogies out of Belfast and Dublin and the captions later mention bringing ten bogies over the bank to Dundalk. The poor coal and the heavy loads took their toll on the engines and, after the war, they needed new fireboxes. The decision was made to replace the round-topped firebox with a Belpaire pattern which should be easier to maintain with the high pressure. The first locomotive to be done was 87 and it got a totally new boiler and firebox from Harland and Wolff in December 1946. This firebox had distinctive protruding ends to the firebox roof stays and this is commented on in the captions which follow. In due course the others received new fireboxes, but the old barrel boiler was retained — 84 in September 1947, 86 in November 1948, 83 in July 1949 and 85 in May 1950. More history of the individual locomotives is given on pages 4-8.

The 1950s saw the Compounds share the heavy main line workings with the new VS class of 1948. However, the gradual onset of dieselisation and particularly the introduction of the BUT railcars in 1957 led to the Compounds being ousted from their regular duties. By 1958 there was little work left for the Compounds.

The last big day for the Compounds was on All-Ireland Football Final day, September 28th 1958. That morning, No. 83 worked 11 bogies from Belfast to Dublin, while No. 86 followed with an 8-bogie train with Kitchen Car and No. 87 was on the 10.15am regular to Dublin which was made up to 10 bogies. The only other active Compound, No. 85 *Merlin*, got in on the act too with a 7-bogie train from Dundalk.

Although the GNR(B) had faced massive closures in 1957, it was not until 1st October 1958 that the Board was finally replaced by the Ulster Transport Authority and Córas Iompair Éireann (CIE). The stencilled letters 'UT' or 'CIE' began to appear on bufferbeams as the Board's assets were divided. So far as the Compounds were concerned, locomotives 84 and 85 passed to CIE and the others (83, 86 and 87) went to the UTA.

The UTA quickly added the fateful red X above the cabside numbers of its three Compounds. This indicated that there was to be no major expenditure on the locomotives; they were to be scrapped when next stopped for heavy repairs.

One of 83's last runs was at Christmas 1958 when she was seen double-heading with 86 on a Dundalk to Belfast passenger train. But both 83 and 87 were auctioned for scrap on 30th March 1960. They had amassed 1,103,858 and 1,005,843 miles in traffic respectively.

The last UTA-owned Compound was 86 but she ran for the last time in the summer of 1960 with a total mileage of 1,181,696. Like all the Compounds, she never strayed from her native main line and the mileage is equivalent to 10,500 journeys between Belfast and Dublin! This most travelled of the three UTA locomotives was auctioned for scrap on 1st May 1961 — but the Compound story wasn't over yet.

By 1958, locomotive 84 had been installed as a stationary boiler alongside the running shed, supplying steam for the new Dundalk Engineering Works. The only obvious differences were a large pipe emerging from just above the smokebox door and a platform welded to the back of the tender to facilitate coaling. No. 84 *Falcon* had acquired the unique boiler with peculiar firebox stays from *Kestrel* and kept it until scrapped in January 1961.

In 1958, No. 85 was in the Works and duly emerged paired with a VS class tender (again, see the captions which follow). No. 85 *Merlin* was usually spare around Dundalk but had a regular turn on the 12.45pm to Dublin and the 5.35pm return working. As late as June 1962 *Merlin* got second-hand tubes from scrapped Woolwich 2-6-0 No. 376. But the revival was short lived and, when steam finished on CIE metals in April 1963, *Merlin* was laid aside at Dundalk. Unfortunately the mileage figures for the two CIE locomotives are not to hand.

Merlin was inspected by the UTA as a possible purchase in early 1963 but they decided on VS No.207 in preference. During the following year, *Merlin* was towed to Dublin Amiens Street and, on 25th April 1964, was moved to Inchicore for scrapping.

The Transport Museum at Witham Street in Belfast, owned by Belfast Corporation, had their eyes on the last of the Compounds. Eventually it was agreed that the Museum would buy the locomotive for £600. Money was tight and the Museum decided to save £200 by not buying the VS tender but rather try for something more suitable from the UTA.

Merlin had buffers and drawgear fitted at the cab end and was hauled back to Amiens Street shed in April 1965 before being moved to Dundalk on 13th May 1965. It was 26th August 1966 before *Merlin* was moved to Adelaide shed but, when that shed closed in November, she was moved again to Lisburn goods store. Nothing is known of the proposed tender purchase from the UTA but a woebegone *Merlin*, minus tender, arrived in a crowded Witham Street museum in late 1969, to take her place alongside a glittering *Dunluce Castle* (NCC 74).

The rest of *Merlin*'s story is told in the photographs and captions which follow.

Dundalk in July 1956 Before detailing *Merlin*'s career in preservation, let's take a moment to look at each of her sisters. No. 83 *Eagle* was the pioneer compound. She was chosen to work the inaugural Belfast - Dublin *Enterprise* on 11th August 1947 and again, on 31st May 1948, she worked the first of the Dublin-based *Enterprises* which was, at one time, to be named *Endeavour*. Here *Eagle* has worked the *Bundoran Express* from Dublin Amiens Street as far as Dundalk. This train brought pilgrims to St. Patrick's Purgatory at Lough Derg, (near Pettigo) and others to the more earthly delights of the Atlantic breakers at Bundoran. Another locomotive, most likely a U class 4-4-0, has already backed on to the other end of the train, ready to work the 105 miles across Ireland in a mere 3 hours 55 minutes — an average speed of 27 mph, but this reaches a giddy 35 mph if you leave out the 55 minutes standing at stations. The balloon water tower at this end of the station has long gone though the semaphore signal survived until fairly recently. The first carriage is a 1928-built K11 Third, the remainder of the set being modern steel panelled stock.

K. R. Photographics C203

Dundalk in May 1957 For this view of 84 *Falcon* in action, we move to the south end of the station where *Falcon*'s train endures the Republic of Ireland Customs, and passengers joining the train here wait at the gate until the job is done. The original Harland and Wolff Belpaire boiler had distinctive protruding ends to the firebox stays and, although built for No. 87, is carried by *Falcon* in this shot. There is a C2 all-First corridor coach next the locomotive which probably indicates that no strengtheners have been added in Belfast. The second coach is in the cream and blue diesel railcar livery. The water tank's support column has two black bands which indicate that "as little water as possible should be taken and only then when absolutely necessary, as the supply is good in winter but uncertain in summer". Now there is only one of these balloon tanks still in use. Note the converted six wheel saloon coach being used as a hut in the background.

T. B. Owen/Colour-Rail (IR 171)

Castlebellingham on 8th September 1962 Here *Merlin* has the 12.45pm from Dundalk to Dublin Amiens Street and the driver awaits the right-away from the guard. The other four Compounds in these first pages are all coupled to the usual Compound tender. Most were built new at Dundalk to accompany the locomotives for, despite Beyer Peacock's publicity and catalogue photographs, they built only the locomotives. The Beyer Peacock builder's photograph of 87, as explained earlier, is a mock-up, showing her coupled to the tender of an SG3 built in 1921. Here, *Merlin* is running with a 4000 gallon tender built in 1948 for a VS class 4-4-0, probably No. 206 *Liffey*. The coach is an L12 class Brake Third built in 1939 and which lasted until 1972. Note too the low-level repeater of the semaphore signal to the left. Castlebellingham is no longer on the railway map.

J. D. FitzGerald.

Belfast (Great Victoria Street) in July 1956 No. 86 *Peregrine* makes a fine sight as she pulls away with the 11.15am to Londonderry (Foyle Road) which she will work as far as Portadown. The leading coach, a K15 70-seater Open Third, has probably been borrowed from an AEC railcar for it is in the blue and cream livery introduced for diesel trains in 1950. To the left, below the Boyne Bridge, can be seen the tail of the 7.15am from Londonderry in Platform 5, which was sacrificed to the buses in March 1962. To its left is the turn-out to the Spion Kop, a pair of short sidings where perishable traffic, including that for the Irish Sea boats was handled. The very individual tower of the Presbyterian Assembly Buildings appears on the left while some of the smaller domes of Belfast City Hall are visible too. Murray's tobacco factory, which gave this station such a distinct aroma, dominates the right-hand boundary of the railway, while in the carriage sidings below are a K3 clerestory-roofed Third and one of the K1 non-corridor Thirds with the low elliptical roofs once so familiar on Lisburn and Portadown locals.

K. R. Photographics No. C387

Adelaide in May 1955 No. 87 *Kestrel* has her coal trimmed forward outside the main running shed at Adelaide, Belfast. Built in 1911, some 1½ miles from the terminus, the shed was a mecca for enthusiasts until its closure in November 1966. Adelaide had the largest allocation of locomotives on the GNR(I), and was unusual in having no turntable. Locomotives were turned on a triangle out of sight in the background of this picture. The boiler on No. 87 was the one first made by Harland and Wolff, and is seen earlier on No. 84 on page 5. The protruding stays high on the side of the firebox can be clearly seen. The locomotive alongside 87 is one of the blue S class inside cylinder 4-4-0s. (See No. 4 in the Colourpoint Transport Series)

T. B. Owen/Colour-Rail IR 172

Queen's Road, Belfast on 21st September 1977 *Merlin* had been resident at the Belfast Transport Museum, Witham Street, since late 1969. At the instigation of the late Lord Dunleath, negotiations were started with the Ulster Folk and Transport Museum with a view to having the locomotive restored to main line running. Preliminary examinations of the boiler seemed hopeful and the next move was to dismantle the locomotive and carry out a detailed assessment. For this, the locomotive was moved to the Engine Works of Harland and Wolff at Queen's Island. In this photograph, 85 has caused something of a traffic jam as she makes for the Works. In this journey she had to cross the Lagan twice, as neither the Dept. of Environment nor the police were satisfied that the bridge over the Bangor line at Dee Street could carry the load. A Northern Ireland Carriers' Scammel provides the motive power.

Harland and Wolff on 26th February 1980 *Merlin*'s boiler has been removed from the frames for work on the firebox to be done. In this view of the frames, the guides that support the reverser rod can be seen on the left near the camera. The main steam pipe carrying steam from the superheater to the high pressure cylinder is visible in the floor of the smokebox (straight ahead). In the cylinder block below, many of the openings have been plugged with wooden blocks. The largest round block indicates where the piston rod emerges from the high pressure cylinder. To the extreme right is evidence of the amount of play in the driving boxes where the back of the right leading driving wheel has worn a crescent-shaped slot in the back of the splasher. At the far end of the slot is the disconnected linkage for working the cylinder drain cocks.

Whitehead on 20th October 1984 No. 85 has been repainted and lined out, but awaits the final dressing of lettering, crests and nameplates. Here the locomotive is in the charge of the Planet diesel, itself something of a curiosity as the only 5 foot 3 inch gauge locomotive produced by Hibberds. The diesel is the regular RPSI shunter at Whitehead. On the running plate, Peter Scott is measuring and checking the valve events as part of setting all three cylinders and valves. The green locomotive behind *Merlin*'s cab is *R. H. Smyth*, an Avonside saddle tank from the Londonderry Port and Harbour Commissioners. The red carriage is ex-GNR L13 Brake Third No. 114, built in 1940 and withdrawn in 1973. *Merlin* was first steamed on 24th December 1984.

The White Harbour on 9th November 1985 On the third of four proving trips, *Merlin* works along the shore of Belfast Lough en route to Antrim. The location is just over a mile from Whitehead, along one of the most photogenic, yet neglected, parts of Ireland's railways. Here *Merlin* has been paired with the 1948-built VS class tender (GNR No. 31). This tender had been attached to 207 *Boyne* when she was bought by the UTA from CIE in June 1963. The Beyer Peacock maker's plate on the tender suggests that this tender was built for 209 *Foyle*. But when *Boyne* went for scrap, the tender escaped and lived to run again, initially behind 171 *Slieve Gullion*. The White Harbour is seen here with its mouth blocked up. Its new owner has since restored it to operational condition. This piece of track was single from its opening until 6th October 1929 when the Kilroot to Whitehead section was doubled. It was singled again in September 1994 due to damage to the sea wall.

Whitehead on 30th June 1986 Following a successful series of running in trips the previous winter, which brought *Merlin* back to the Great Northern briefly, all was set for her debut working public trains. The locomotive was officially launched at Whitehead on this day with assembled guests from the railway companies, local authorities, tourist bodies, the shipyard and other friends of the Society. Lord Dunleath himself drove *Merlin* through a red tape to mark the occasion and several detonators announced another remarkable achievement — No. 85 *Merlin* was back! Here Lord Dunleath (centre) poses with the RPSI footplate crew of Irwin Pryce (left) and Paul Newell, RPSI Locomotive Running Officer. Irwin had privately organised, funded and supplied the replica nameplates in memory of his father, the late Irwin Pryce, Senior, who had been an Inspector at Great Victoria Street.

Top of the Bank on 13th September 1986 Another shot from that fateful day when 85's main line future was decided (see front cover). The location is a classic — half a mile south of Cloghogue Chapel and the start of the final cutting to the top of the bank at milepost 65½. If you can, do compare this with the frontispiece of the May 1937 Railway Magazine which is an O. S. Nock photograph of 84 *Falcon*, with round-topped firebox, of course, storming up to the summit with 10 bogies including a dining car. The train was the Up Limited Mail but there is nothing limited about it that I can see! And there was nothing limited about 85's performance here either — she looked and sounded great. This was the first Compound in this part of the world for twenty five years! The carriage immediately behind the locomotive in GNR A5 Saloon No. 50, here restored to the GNR mahogany livery. In 1953 No. 50 had acted as the Royal Saloon for the visit of Queen Elizabeth II to N. Ireland after her Coronation. Between its construction in 1911 and the demise of the GNR(I) in 1958, No. 50 had been the Directors' Saloon. Its last important duty, as UTA No. 150, was to convey round the system the men who drew up the Benson Report which recommended the closure of both routes to Derry.

Drogheda on 13th September 1986 Our front cover and the previous photograph were also taken on this day and I have already described the circumstances of the trip and its significance. Here, after arriving in Drogheda, *Merlin* has just shunted the stock into the middle road before going to turn and get ready for the homeward run. With the engine in blue livery and the only coach visible in GNR livery, there is little to give this away as a 1986 view and not something from 1956 or even earlier. A week later, on its next run to Dublin, such a shot was no longer possible because Merlin was fitted with a small deflector plate, mounted between and above the safety valves, for working under the overhead electrification wires in the Dublin area. This is just visible in the next picture. But on 13th September, all was well with the world — God was in His heaven and there was a Compound on the main line!

Dublin Connolly on 20th September 1986 Following the success of the trial to Drogheda the week before, *Merlin* set off for Dublin with eight bogies the very next week. Amiens Street was renamed Connolly in 1966, but the old name is still used just as much as the new one. Seeing a Compound back in Amiens Street, after an absence of over twenty years, was another milestone in Irish railway history. On arrival in Dublin, the locomotive was surrounded by crowds, some recalling the last time they saw a Compound here and many more savouring the experience for the first time. The crowds eventually drifted away and, for once, I was pleased that the shunt took so long to get under way. The delay gave me the chance to photograph the train at the buffers under the great overall roof. The way the light is hitting the carriages disguises the fact that only the first coach is in GNR livery. The black and white tiles are a CIE addition and there is just a glimpse of a 071 class diesel electric locomotive above *Merlin*'s chimney. The deflector plate over the safety valves is just visible silhouetted against the sign for Platform 4. The great pile of mailbags on the platform is a reminder of a traffic that has all but deserted the modern railway.

Glarryford on 18th July 1987 By now 171 *Slieve Gullion* was back in action, so *Merlin* had to give up the 3500 gallon tender and revert to the 4000 gallon VS tender. *Merlin* had worked to Dublin and back as part of the 1987 big tour, the *Lough Gill* to Sligo. In Dublin that evening there was a glimpse of past glories when 171 met 85 at the platform ends. Then 85 had two runs on the NCC — one to Coleraine on the Monday of the big tour and then a solo *Portrush Flyer* on 18th July. Here *Merlin* spins along in fine style, in the mid fifties, alongside the River Maine just south of Glarryford, with the return working. For the technically minded, this is a panned shot with a 200 mm lens and an exposure of a sixtieth of a second at f5.6. The film was Kodachrome 64 — as it was for most of my photographs in this book. Some of the early ones are on Kodachrome 25 while the next picture was on Kodachrome 200 as an insurance against a dull day.

Belfast Central on 11th August 1987 Northern Ireland Railways celebrated the fortieth anniversary of the *Enterprise* with as near a replica of 1947 as possible. The engine was *Merlin* rather than 83, but the 7-bogie load, the departure time and the timings were identical to the first run in 1947. Denis Grimshaw, then NIR's General Manager InterCity, worked out the very detailed arrangements with the help of NIR's ever-resourceful Locomotive Inspector, Frank Dunlop. For some days before, 85 and train were at the Central Service Depot having both interior and exterior cleaned — and cleaned again. The whole ensemble was immaculate and won much praise for all concerned from the trainful of important guests. Here *Merlin* and train stand ready and the tender gets a final top-up from a carriage watering hose. The three leading vehicles are ex-GNR(I) — Brake Third No. 114; Open Third No. 9; and the Directors' Saloon No. 50. NIR provided new headboards, copied from an original retrieved from Adelaide by Harry Martin. All went well and *Merlin* rolled into Connolly just ahead of the $2\frac{1}{4}$ hour timing. Another of Lord Dunleath's dreams had come true.

16

Top: **Dublin Shed on 12th September 1987** A shot that is almost timeless. Apart from a couple of electrification poles, this could have been 1958. A beaming Bobby Quail, another of the heroes of *Merlin*'s return to the main line, brings his locomotive back to the turntable at Amiens Street after another successful run up the main line.

Left: **Drogheda on 12th September 1987** There is a 15 mph slack across the Boyne Viaduct and through the curved platforms at Drogheda, but once clear of that there is a fairly straight road the rest of the way to Dublin. On this occasion, just as the last carriage cleared the footbridge, the driver heaved the regulator wide and *Merlin*'s chimney erupted noisily. The locomotive had steam to spare, kept its feet and began to accelerate confidently, that heavy exhaust thumping into the air and echoing back off the cutting and trees with every purposeful quarter turn of the wheels. In the left background, the branch to Navan and Kingscourt (and, at one time, Oldcastle) diverges just short of Drogheda's new, flat-roofed and rather ugly signal cabin, a 1978 replacement for the old North and South cabins. The twin goods stores behind have since been demolished.

Boyne Viaduct on 12th September 1987 After a water stop at Drogheda, *Merlin* sets out for home with new heart. This viaduct, with its 550 foot long metal spans, stands about 100 feet above the River Boyne. It was rebuilt in 1932, partly to accommodate the Compounds. Here the dip in the exhaust clearly shows where the driver has shut the regulator before opening it wide to get the locomotive over into compounding and then closing it to suit the job in hand. Judging by the black smoke, the fireman is hard at work building up his fire for the next five miles to the top of Kellystown bank, most of it at 1 in 177.

Later on the same run, *Merlin* is just short of the land border between the Irish Republic and N. Ireland at Milepost 59½ which also marks where NIR meets Irish Rail. With almost 4 miles of climbing behind her, *Merlin* is nearing the top of 2 miles at 1 in 100 but there are another 4 miles to the dip at Adavoyle at only slightly easier grades. Here the low evening sun fills the compartments of the leading coach and picks out the carriage roof boards while the fireman is again busy with the shovel.

At the foot of Slieve Gullion on 26th September 1987 Another north-bound 9-bogie train is seen here about Milepost 64½, a mile short of the summit, in the townland of Newtown. *Merlin* has the bulk of the work behind her. After passing Adavoyle she has tackled a further two miles of climbing and here she is on the final 1 in 120. The dramatic lighting comes from a setting sun which has just dipped below the hill in the right background. That hill is the foot of Slieve Gullion which rises to 1894 feet and dominates the line for many miles. A fortnight earlier and this shot would have been (and was!) straight into a dying but strong evening sun. Note that the headboard is Dublin to Belfast — a replica of a board carried by some Dublin-based locomotives but rarely photographed.

Whitehead on 11th October 1987 *Merlin* finished a busy year with a Larne Lough tour — then the traditional end to the running season when the *Steam Enterprises* operated. The train has worked from Central Station to Larne Harbour via Lisburn, Antrim and York Road. As usual on this trip, the train made a boat-train style non-stop run from the Harbour to York Road before finally retiring to Whitehead. Here *Merlin* has just cleared Whitehead (NIR) station at speed and is blowing off impatiently for the double track run ahead. The deflector plate, mentioned earlier, is spreading the steam left and right. Late on this sharp October afternoon, the promenade, built by the Belfast and Northern Counties Railway, is clearly visible though nothing remains of the landing stage or the sand imported — by rail of course — from Portrush, to make a strand along the seafront. The furthest point is Black Head lighthouse.

Limerick Junction on 13th May 1989 The *Mount Brandon* was *Merlin*'s only excursion (at the time of writing!) off NIR or ex-GNR metals. On the Saturday, she worked a set of Irish Rail Cravens from Dublin (Kingsbridge) — now Heuston — to Mallow. There the tour participants transferred to the Mullingar set of coaches, hauled by 2-6-4T No. 4, for the run to Tralee. *Merlin* followed and worked a train of tourists to Killarney for Irish Rail in the process. Here we see *Merlin* reversing the Cravens to the platform after a servicing stop at Limerick Junction, propelling the train through the famous cross-over that is such a landmark. The 4000 gallon tender had given some trouble on the 1988 *Flyers*, so *Merlin* was again paired with No. 171's tender (No. 12). The Cravens were built in 1964-67 and were the first integral steel constructed coaches on CIE.

Bleach Green Viaduct on 5th August 1989 *Merlin* gets the 57th (!) *Portrush Flyer* excursion off to a rousing start as she pounds across the 630 foot long viaduct and up the 1 in 76 of the loop line between Whiteabbey and Mossley. The train headboard — raised brass letters on a red ground — is always carried low on *Merlin* rather than obscure the chimney. In other years, this weekend would be about the middle of the *Flyer* season, but NIR was to charter the train (see next picture) and the whole *Flyer* programme was moved forward, making this the third and final train of the 1989 season. Away to the left are the waters of Belfast Lough with the County Down coast beyond.

PS: With reference to the graffitti, does anyone know if Billy and Martha are still together?

Ormeau Road Bridge, Belfast, on 10th August 1989 The Ulster Railway opened between Belfast and Lisburn on 12th August 1839. It was Ireland's second railway and Ulster's first. To commemorate a century and a half of train travel, NIR organised a series of events collectively known as "Ulster 150". NIR chartered *Merlin* and train to operate rush hour trains to Belfast from Larne, Antrim, Bangor and Portadown on successive mornings. Everyone had a day off on the Friday and the celebrations culminated with a series of eight round trips between Belfast and Lisburn on the Saturday. The departure times were similar to those of 1839, though only the first train of the day called at Dunmurry, which was the only intermediate station in 1839. Here *Merlin* passes the site of the Belfast Central Railway's Ormeau Road halt (closed on 11th November 1885) with the 08.14am from Portadown. The train served Lurgan, Moira, Lisburn and Botanic en route to Central and the locomotive headlamp code (one lamp at the chimney) correctly indicates a stopping passenger train.

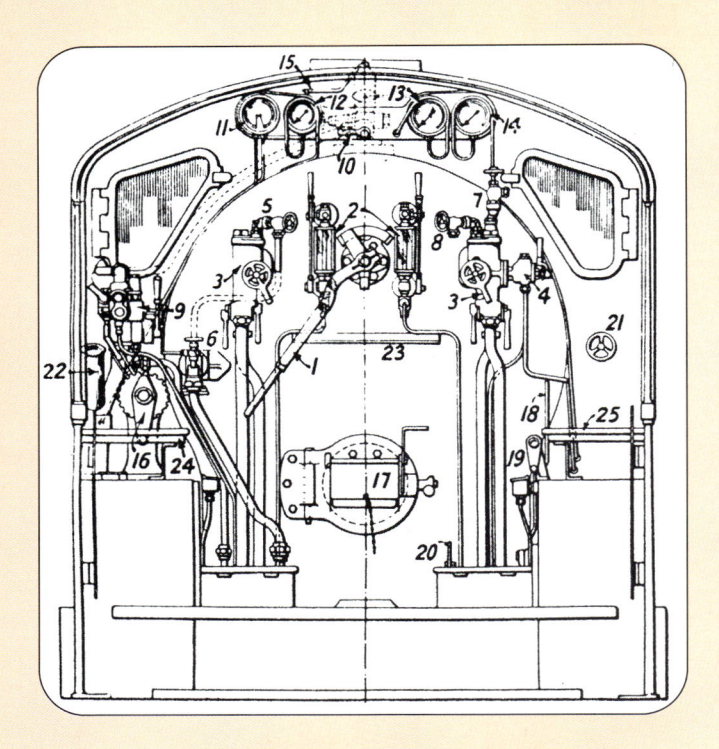

Arrangement of Footplate Fittings
V Class three cylinder compound locomotive, GNR(I)

1 Regulator handle
2 Water-gauge glasses
3 Combination injectors
4 Steam sanding cock
5 Steam heating cock
6 Steam heating reducing valve
7 Coal watering cock
8 Tube cleaning cock
9 'Dreadnought' vacuum ejector
10 Vacuum ejector steam cock handle
11 Vacuum gauge
12 Steam heating gauge
13 Boiler pressure gauge
14 Receiving gauge
15 Whistle lever
16 Reversing handle
17 Firedoor
18 Cylinder drain-cock lever
19 Front damper lever
20 Back damper lever
21 Blower wheel
22 Staff holder
23 Kettle tray
24 Driver's seat
25 Fireman's seat

Reproduced from *Locomotive Management*, 1948

Whitehead on 23rd June 1984 This is a view of the cab of No. 85 *Merlin* and should be compared with the diagram alongside. The principal difference is, of course, that the drawing is of an original cab with the round-topped firebox whereas *Merlin* now has a Belpaire firebox. As a result, the triangular windows of 1932 became rectangular ones in 1950. One curiosity must be the staff holder (no. 22 in the drawing). I have often wondered (and still do) how on earth this came to be here since the Compounds were banned from all the single track lines where staffs were in use. Did someone take the drawing of a PP cab and work from that? And why was it allowed to remain? Was it ever used between Drogheda and Mosney perhaps? Maybe it had a role in smuggling days! Any ideas?